CORNELL WOMEN LEADING THE WAY IN SCIENCE, TECHNOLOGY, AND ENGINEERING

WALL OF WONDER

MADELINE DUBELIER, CATHERINE GURECKY, AND ABIGAIL MACALUSO
PORTRAITS BY DAVID ROSS JANSEN

In September 2019, only one of Forbes' one hundred innovative leaders was a woman ("America's Most Innovative Leaders"). Throughout history, women have been breaking boundaries in technology, but recognition has been few and far between. Lack of recognition has left young girls and aspiring women without role models, thus contributing to the gender gap in technical fields. With this book, we hope to increase visibility of female leaders and showcase the breadth of work women have accomplished through technical backgrounds. We believe diversity of thought is critical to innovation and is something to be celebrated.

As graduating seniors of Cornell University's College of Engineering, we set out to commemorate Cornell alumnae who inspire us during our transition to impactful careers in technology. We are confident that these stories will continue to inspire us throughout our lives and, moreover, inspire the next generation of scientists and engineers.

Special thanks to the Cornell University section of the Society of Women Engineers (SWE) for providing us with a platform for change. We could not have accomplished this publication nor many other endeavors without the support of SWE and Cornell at large.

Madeline Dubelier, Catherine Gurecky, Abigail Macaluso
Cornell University College of Engineering, Class of 2020

CONTENTS

PRENTHIS DAVIS AGUILAR

B.S. Mechanical and Aerospace Engineering, Cornell University (1986)
M.S. Systems Engineering, Stevens Institute of Technology (2013)

Prenthis Davis Aguilar dreamed of becoming an astronaut from a young age. Her love for reading and science fiction transported her childhood mind to outer space and eventually led her to engineering. Prenthis' high school advisors provided invaluable mentorship and encouraged her to challenge herself with studies in STEM. Coming to Cornell University was a difficult adjustment for Prenthis because she was accustomed to being one of the "smartest kids" in school. At Cornell, Prenthis was surrounded by talented, like-minded students and found herself working harder than ever to achieve her aspirations.

After graduating from Cornell, Prenthis worked to improve satellite communication with RCA Astro-Electronics. She enjoyed expanding her skillset across the technological landscape and made subsequent transitions to AT&T, General Motors, and IBM. In 2003, she landed at Northrop Grumman where she has worked on a diverse portfolio transversing the electronic, satellite, and aerospace industries. While at Northrop Grumman, she completed her master's degree in Systems Engineering. Today, she continues with the company as a Verification Engineering Manager, leading environmental qualification to ensure products are functional, reliable, and safe before their release.

Prenthis is passionate about paving the way for women who come after her. Her experiences at Cornell and throughout industry encouraged her to start her own website, *Lopolopo*. This website offers a place for women of all backgrounds to become educated about the electronics and technologies of today. She encourages every woman to be aware of technological advancements because they are integral to the daily workings of society.

During her years at Cornell University, Dr. Rosemarie Aurigemma was exposed to all that science had to offer. She was a Biology major and conducted research in the veterinary school. She loved school days when students dissected animals, and the anatomy section of her encyclopedia fascinated her. It was this introduction to laboratory studies that made her want to become a scientist. She applied to graduate school to study retroviruses, a group of viruses that cause cancer.

Once in industry, Rosemarie transitioned to working in drug development to treat cancer and metabolic diseases. She became the Program Director of Developmental Therapeutics at the National Cancer Institute and worked to develop anticancer therapies. Over the course of eight years in this laborious, yet fast-paced environment, Rosemarie found her vocational drive and was able to move seven products into clinical trials. She later joined the National Institute of Allergy and Infectious Diseases as Chief of Drug Development and drove innovation on drugs and biologic therapies for infectious disease epidemics, such as the Ebola outbreak and antibiotic resistant bacteria. In 2017, she returned to the National Cancer Institute as Deputy Associate Director of Developmental Therapeutics. She is now working in the burgeoning immunotherapy field with a focus on pediatric cancers and difficult-to-treat tumors.

Rosemarie also shines light on the importance of having more women in the field of translational and clinical research, particularly in oncology. Rosemarie has been lucky to have worked with many highly accomplished women in her career, sharing that this community brings much-needed perspective to their highly diverse patient population.

ROSEMARIE AURIGEMMA, PH.D.

B.S. Biology, Cornell University (1982)
Ph.D. Microbiology, Colorado State University (1989)

> Find the helpers in life; even if something seems too difficult, find someone to help you, and you can conquer anything.

ANDREA J. BERMAN, PH.D.

B.S. Biological Sciences, Cornell University (2001)
Ph.D. Molecular Biophysics and Biochemistry, Yale University (2007)

"[In research], there's nothing more exciting than seeing something that no one else has seen in the entire world."

Dr. Andrea Berman has always loved science. She takes inspiration from her father who was a science teacher and an electrical engineer. Andrea was a Biology student at Cornell University and conducted research in the chemistry department. Later, she continued her academic journey studying Molecular Biophysics at Yale University with a focus in understanding how genomes are copied. After graduating with her Ph.D., she moved to Colorado where she was a postdoctoral fellow and studied how the ends of chromosomes are maintained. After interviewing for a position in industry, Andrea quickly realized that industry was not her calling and set her sights on a career in academia. Andrea shares that this process was not easy and notes that she faced a lot of rejection along the way. Applying to over sixty positions, Andrea received eleven interviews and four offers. She remained resilient, and at the end of this long process, Andrea secured an assistant professorship at the University of Pittsburgh where she continues to investigate the complex functions of cells.

Andrea has had great success and regards many of the women who went before her as trailblazers. While completing her advanced degree, there were only two women with Ph.D.'s among her thirty laboratory colleagues. Those two women showed Andrea that it was possible for her to succeed in the field of molecular biophysics. Her advisor's wife and tenured women in her current department showed her that it is possible to accomplish great career milestones while having a family. Today, Andrea takes her job as a mentor to graduate students very seriously. She writes, "My mentors taught me to be a rigorous, but kind scientist. These characteristics have been instrumental in training graduate students to be thoughtful, collaborative, and careful scientists."

In eighth grade, Danielle (Vollmar) Breezy's class received a special visit from the Philadelphia NBC Chief Meteorologist, Glenn "Hurricane" Schwartz. Danielle was a strong student in science and math, but she attributes this experience to her catching "the weather bug." This weather bug stuck with Danielle, leading her to pursue a degree in Atmospheric Sciences at Cornell University. While at Cornell, she was the first female meteorologist to write for the Cornell Daily Sun and commuted to surrounding towns to regularly appear on local weather programs.

After graduation, Danielle's TV meteorologist positions led her to Maryland, Oklahoma, Texas, and Massachusetts. In 2016, Danielle married Joe Breezy, giving her a very fitting last name for her profession. That same year she moved to Tennessee to become the Chief Meteorologist for Nashville's local ABC station. Only eight percent of Chief Meteorologist jobs in the United States are held by women. Because of this, Danielle has faced a lot of challenges related to her gender. Danielle has learned much from the negative comments, poor treatment, and antiquated standards she has confronted. In reflecting on her current leadership style, she shares, "I'm still very strong and direct, but I also like to be kind. At the end of the day, if we are nice to one another, the world is a better place."

In addition to keeping citizens informed regarding the weather, Danielle believes it is her responsibility to give back to her community, something she's carried with her everywhere she has lived. Danielle visits local schools every week to share her love of meteorology and, more generally, science with younger students. Danielle shares, "I want these kids, all of them, to get that weather bug. If one of them wants to go into math and science, that's great."

DANIELLE (VOLLMAR) BREEZY

B.S. Atmospheric Sciences, Cornell University (2006)

"I got the opportunity of a lifetime to be a Chief Meteorologist in Nashville. It was my dream to do it by 40, and I did it at 31."

REGINA CLEWLOW, PH.D.

B.S. Computer Science, Cornell University (2001)
M.Eng. Civil and Environmental Engineering, Cornell University (2002)
Ph.D. Engineering Systems, Massachusetts Institute of Technology (2012)

Tackling environmental issues has been Dr. Regina Clewlow's passion since childhood. A Silicon Valley native, she began making change in her community by starting her high school's first recycling program. While a Master of Engineering student at Cornell University, she founded Engineers without Frontiers USA, now known as Engineers for a Sustainable World. She remained the organization's executive director for six years, leading a mission to solve global sustainability crises. She then went on to earn her Ph.D. in Engineering Systems with an emphasis on climate energy systems and transportation.

After completing her degrees, Regina pursued several fellowships and research appointments in the field of transportation, developing software to model public transportation flow. It was during this period that Regina co-founded Populus with a colleague from University of California Berkeley. As the Chief Executive Officer of Populus, Regina oversees a company that helps cities manage the future of mobility - enabling cities to make data-driven decisions to improve safety, equity, and efficiency.

Regina is a trailblazer in the transportation industry, but her journey was not short of challenges. Raising funding for Populus as a female in Silicon Valley, where only 2.8 percent of venture capital went to female founding teams in 2019, was not an easy feat. Committed to her vision, Regina has grown Populus to over seventy cities on four continents since 2017, and it is now a leading platform for city departments of transportation to plan for the future. She has demonstrated Populus is a leader in its field and encourages all young women to pursue their passions despite the inevitable hurdles.

When choosing a college major, Joanna Dai was inspired by her father, a mechanical engineer, and was determined to become an engineer because of the challenge and prestige associated with the profession. Joanna's strong desire to seek challenges is a common thread throughout her career.

After graduating from Cornell University with a degree in Electrical and Computer Engineering, Joanna transitioned into finance, working for J.P. Morgan on the trading floor. She loved the fast-paced nature of investment banking and although the industry was dominated by men, Joanna retained a positive perspective: "[This culture] grants you a platform to stand out for yourself." However, after eight years in banking, Joanna desired a more creative and tangibly-oriented profession.

After spending years in a business formal environment, Joanna had become accustomed to working long days in uncomfortable and stuffy suiting. She saw a gap in the market for workwear that looked tailored and smart but was as comfortable as her yoga pants. She took a sabbatical to pursue this idea, taking classes at the London College of Fashion and interning with Emilia Wickstead. After a year of learning, Joanna founded Dai, a performance womenswear brand based in London. Initially, Joanna used her savings to support the business, attending trunk shows to gather as much feedback as possible. A writer for *The Times*, a British national newspaper, discovered the Dai collection at a trunk show and wrote an article, "How to get dressed: the perfect trousers," naming Joanna's trousers the best in fashion. The pants sold out immediately. Joanna has been growing her business ever since and plans to open offices in New York City in the near future.

JOANNA DAI

B.S. Electrical and Computer Engineering, Cornell University (2008)

ERICA FISCHER, PH.D., P.E.

B.S. Civil and Environmental Engineering, Cornell University (2007)
Ph.D. Civil and Environmental Engineering, Purdue University (2015)

"Be yourself. When you're bringing your unique perspectives, that's when we'll be able to truly solve a problem."

Dr. Erica Fischer is a professor of Civil and Construction Engineering at Oregon State University. She researches innovative, affordable, and accessible approaches to the design of civil infrastructure with the goal of making cities more resilient to disasters. However, as she explains it, Erica's path to this point was not linear: "When I was younger, I wish I'd known it was okay to not know what you wanted to do with your life." Up until her third year at Cornell University, Erica was a Biological Engineering student and had never envisioned graduate school. Switching majors and eventually pursuing her Ph.D. were difficult decisions, but those decisions have led to a career she is passionate about - a career that "aims to help humanity by making communities safer."

Over the course of her career, Erica has investigated how areas in Haiti, Italy, and Mexico City as well as Napa and Paradise, California have performed in earthquakes and fires. She has also worked as a practicing engineer in New York City and Seattle. Her work has spanned many types of disasters, but all of her projects are united by humanitarian efforts. Erica realizes that the real engineering challenges are centered on the user experience and appreciates the breadth of opportunities and humanitarian classes she was exposed to at Cornell. As she says, "My undergraduate engineering courses gave me the foundational skill set to tackle diverse problems."

From graduate school into her career, Erica has been heavily involved in the Earthquake Engineering Research Institute; she now holds a spot on the Institute's board. She also co-founded the Virtual Earthquake Reconnaissance Team, a team of roughly two hundred individuals in disaster-related fields from around the globe who gather data and create reports on how to respond to earthquake situations. Throughout all of her endeavors, Erica remains inspired by the ability of civil engineers to blur the line between social science and urban planning.

Dr. Jessica Baker Flechtner rode horses as a child, and, for as long as she can remember, she dreamed of becoming a veterinarian. With these aspirations in mind, Jessica pursued her undergraduate studies in Animal Science and then applied to Cornell University's Doctor of Veterinary Medicine program. Unfortunately, Jessica was not accepted. Not ready to give up, she began a job as a research technician at Cornell and ultimately pursued a master's degree in the veterinary school. Jessica soon found that she loved her research on the female horse's unique immune system during pregnancy. This work inspired her to transfer to a Ph.D. program at Cornell in which she completed her doctorate in Cellular Immunology in only three and a half years before continuing to a post-doctoral position at Harvard Medical School.

Although her initial career dreams did not come to fruition, Jessica's perseverance and positivity have led her to a motivating career. Following her passion to help patients, Jessica left academia to pursue a career in the biotechnology industry. She now serves as Chief Scientific Officer (CSO) at Genocea Biosciences and leads a team to develop novel immunotherapies and vaccines.

Jessica's ultimate advice: "Look for the open window when the door is closed. You either learn from failure and grow, or you can let it consume you." Even today as CSO, Jessica finds herself questioning her abilities. However, she always emphasizes a growth mindset and stays motivated by the opportunity to save patients' lives. She hopes to spread the message to young children that science is rewarding and can take them places that they never imagined.

JESSICA BAKER FLECHTNER, PH.D.

B.S. Animal Science, Cornell University (1993)
Ph.D. Cellular Immunology, Cornell University (2000)

"The first time that a vaccine my team and I created went into a patient and helped them was one of the most rewarding times of my professional life."

MALIKA GRAYSON, PH.D.

B.S. Physics, Adelphi University (2011)
M.S. Mechanical Engineering, Cornell University (2014)
Ph.D. Mechanical Engineering, Cornell University (2016)

" I remind myself that I'm not being a STEM advocate for me, but I am doing it so the next woman, the next girl that looks like me, knows that it can be done. "

Dr. Malika Grayson grew up on the island of Trinidad and Tobago with her large, loving family. From a young age, she was encouraged to pursue traditional professions in science or engineering. At the time, Malika did not know what a career in engineering entailed, but she did know that she wanted to understand how things work. Malika was a Physics major during her undergraduate years and learned about mechanical engineering through a research experience. In the research laboratory, Malika was able to see the physics equations she had learned about in the classroom being applied to real world challenges. With her curiosity ignited, she began to look into doctoral programs, ultimately leading her to Cornell University.

Malika never imagined that earning her doctorate from Cornell would be as difficult as it was. She is the second Black woman to have graduated from Cornell with a Ph.D. in Mechanical Engineering. She was able to find her support system through the Diversity Programs in Engineering organization and her faculty advisor. With the death of her advisor during her graduate studies, Malika questioned if she should finish. Thankfully, the community she had built at Cornell supported her, guiding her through graduation and the start of her career at Northrop Grumman as a systems engineer in one of the company's top rotational programs.

Today, Malika is an Applications Portfolio Manager. She works to ensure that the business applications within the company's portfolio are not just the best fit financially but also aligned with the company's needs. Her career has given her unique experiences that have helped motivate her passion for encouraging minorities to pursue advanced degrees and careers in STEM. She authors a blog, *Black Girls Guide to Grad School*, and mentors female undergraduates by reviewing their personal statements for graduate school applications. She holds speaking engagements on topics that range from imposter syndrome to conquering graduate school. In her hometown, Malika has established a scholarship for young women who want to pursue degrees in STEM.

When Dr. Susan Hakkarainen was ten years old, her dad began to gift her electronics kits with strobe lights and various devices to build. She recalls quickly completing each kit with excitement. Her interest and enthusiasm for electronics were fostered by her parents who were pioneers in the lighting industry. They founded Lutron Electronics Company in 1961 with the invention of the first electronic dimmer. Now, Lutron is a global company that produces dimmers, lighting control, and automated shading systems as well as smart LED bulbs.

Upon completing her doctorate, Susan began working as a research scientist for Toshiba in Japan as part of an exchange program. As a result of that experience, she had the opportunity to launch Lutron's Japan sales operation, allowing her to explore sales, marketing, and business development from an international perspective. With a diverse skill set, Susan moved from operating a business unit to managing overall communications and marketing. In 2015, Susan became the Co-Chairman and Co-Chief Executive Officer (CEO) of Lutron Electronics.

As Chairman and CEO, in addition to her operating responsibilities, Susan leads initiatives in long-term strategic areas such as digitalization, big data, user experience, and overall company strategy. She continues her parents' pioneering spirit by ensuring her company is investing in innovation and searching for new technologies to improve the way people live and work. Susan is heavily involved in Lutron's Product Design Group, which not only looks at aesthetics but also new ways to enhance the user experience. She leads continuous technology and business development while maintaining Lutron's core principles. Susan writes, "To successfully do corporate innovation, it is important to get others to be part of the process. I learned that having a good idea is only ten percent of the job. The other ninety percent of the job is getting people to understand, embrace, and take ownership of the idea."

SUSAN HAKKARAINEN, PH.D.

B.S. Electrical Engineering, Cornell University (1982)
M.Eng. Electrical Engineering, Cornell University (1983)
Ph.D. Nuclear Engineering, Massachusetts Institute of Technology (1989)

KAREN HAVENSTRITE, PH.D.

B.S. Chemical Engineering, Cornell University (2005)
Ph.D. Chemical Engineering, Stanford University (2011)
M.B.A., Stanford University (2015)

"There's always a path to go where you want to go; you just have to find it."

As a child, Dr. Karen Havenstrite was exposed to industrial scale chemistry by her father who worked in mining. Inspired and curious, Karen took her interests in chemistry outside of the high school classroom and built her own battery at home. This creative spirit did not end here, as Karen continued on to study Chemical Engineering at Cornell University where she was highly involved in research. Her love for laboratory studies led her to pursue a Ph.D. at Stanford University and explore the regenerative properties of stem cells. At Stanford, Karen realized that her favorite aspect of doing research is the opportunity to build new products. The entrepreneurial spirit resonated with Karen, and she knew that she could use her scientific background to create products that would better peoples' lives. She didn't want a big company culture, so she forged her own path and created exactly what she wanted.

In 2011, Karen co-founded Tangible Science, a company which designs materials to make contact lenses more comfortable. Karen has served as Chief Technical Officer since the company's inception and took Tangible's core technology from ideation to market. However, the path to Tangible's success was not always easy. Karen admits that there were points when others believed the company would not survive, but the team's perseverance proved worthwhile. In 2013, Karen returned to university to earn her M.B.A. from Stanford Business School, an opportunity that expanded her skillset to grow the business.

Of her work, Karen remarks, "I love what I do. People think of STEM as being so hard and complicated, but it can be an opportunity to apply creativity to solve problems." As a working mom, Karen has faced a new realm of challenges but applies an engineering mindset to manage her work-life balance and has found the experience extremely rewarding.

Priscilla Hung has spent her thirty-year career in the software industry. Surprisingly, as a child in Hong Kong, she had dreams of becoming an artist. Priscilla was a trained pianist and skilled ballerina, but her parents strongly encouraged her to consider fields such as engineering, law, or medicine. Priscilla shares that she has a fear of blood and wasn't interested in spending years in school, so she landed on engineering by process of elimination. Although engineering and computing were not her initial interests, Priscilla has had a fulfilling and successful career in technology and loves her work.

Today, Priscilla is the Chief Operating Officer at Guidewire Software in the San Francisco Bay Area. Priscilla shares, "The biggest challenge I've always faced is I don't look like what an executive would look like." Priscilla has often had to work harder than others to make her voice heard and has had to redefine what a "typical" executive looks and acts like. These experiences have caused Priscilla to realize the importance of supporting other women on her teams and fostering a community where women can feel comfortable asking for advice and sharing challenges.

In the pursuit of discovering her career ambitions, Priscilla worked for many companies in a variety of positions. While these transitions were often daunting and challenging, Priscilla recommends, "Have the courage to change jobs and go find your passion. Otherwise, you'll become complacent. Life is short, and you can miss a big opportunity. Finally, nothing can replace hard work."

PRISCILLA HUNG

B.A. Computer Science, Mills College (1988)
M.Eng. Operations Research and Information Engineering, Cornell University (1989)

"The common thread over my career is I've never stopped looking for things that I'm passionate about."

ANDREA IPPOLITO

B.S. Biological Engineering, Cornell University (2006)
M. Eng. Biomedical Engineering, Cornell University (2007)
M.S. Engineering and Management, Massachusetts Institute of Technology (2012)

"That is what I love about my journey, it is not linear. I have worked in amazing environments: large companies, government, higher-ed, and start-ups."

Andrea Ippolito was extremely lucky to have parents who were both engineers; they exposed her to STEM in many ways. Andrea comments on this access, "It was everything from going to science camp to talking about it at the dinner table. I was extremely lucky to have that much support." It was through these experiences that Andrea began to appreciate how technology could be used to solve problems.

Andrea attended Cornell University for undergraduate studies in Biological Engineering and then for her Master of Engineering in Biomedical Engineering. She served as the Co-President of the Society of Women Engineers (SWE) during her time at Cornell. She recalls, "When I was having trouble in class, SWE gave me a chance to thrive." After graduation, Andrea landed at Boston Scientific working in the medical device industry. While in this job, she started to recognize her strengths of bringing people within the organization together and improving the pace of R&D by building innovation ecosystems.

Andrea went on to pursue a master's degree at Massachusetts Institute of Technology, involving herself in many hackathons and entrepreneurial ventures in the digital healthcare field, including co-founding the start-up Smart Scheduling (acquired by athenahealth in 2016). This passion for solving healthcare-related problems took her to Washington, D.C. where she served as a Presidential Innovation Fellow under the White House Office of Science and Technology Policy at the Department of Veterans Affairs. In this role, Andrea worked to establish an innovation and investment program called the Innovators Network to better serve Veterans and their families. Andrea shares one of her biggest takeaways from these experiences in healthcare and entrepreneurship, "It is so important to take time to get to know people, their needs, and where they're coming from." Today, Andrea has a teaching position at Cornell University and continues to pursue entrepreneurial ventures in the healthcare field.

Dr. Ann L. Lee was drawn to science by her high school biology teacher and the excitement of a botany research project she completed while a high school intern at the U.S. Department of Agriculture. She used that research project to compete in and win local and even international science fairs. These hands-on experiences cultivated Ann's love of scientific inquiry. Ann pursued these interests and majored in Chemical Engineering at Cornell University, choosing this major with an eagerness for a challenge.

When reminiscing about her career options, Ann mentions, "I was very motivated to use my chemical engineering background to make the world a better place, and I chose to work in healthcare to help patients." Her first job was at Merck Research Labs where she developed vaccines to save infant lives. Advancing through several project and managerial leadership roles over fourteen years, Ann became Global Head of Chemical Technology and Engineering. She enjoyed the challenges of building and starting up new facilities and processes around the world and improving the efficiency of pharmaceutical production. Most of all, Ann enjoyed working with talented people and learning about their different cultures.

Ann's next challenge brought her to Genentech where she led all teams that developed processes and technologies to produce new medicines to treat cancer and other diseases. After twelve years, Ann became fascinated by the new field of cell and gene therapy, and she joined Juno Therapeutics which was acquired by Bristol Myers Squibb. Today, Ann is Head of Cell Therapy Development and Operations at Bristol Myers Squibb. Their main goal is to re-engineer a patient's own unique T-cells to attack cancer cells. Her teams are developing new processes and technologies, manufacturing the CAR T-cells, designing new facilities, and building the global supply chain to deliver these new medicines, giving hope to patients.

ANN L. LEE, PH.D.

B.S. Chemical Engineering, Cornell University (1983)
M.S. Chemical Engineering, Yale University (1985)
Ph.D. Chemical Engineering, Yale University (1989)

"Don't be afraid to take on new challenges, keep believing in yourself, and remember— chemical engineers can do anything.

MARGARET MARTONOSI, PH.D.

B.S. Electrical Engineering, Cornell University (1986)
M.S. Electrical Engineering, Stanford University (1987)
Ph.D. Electrical Engineering, Stanford University (1994)

Dr. Margaret Martonosi grew up with STEM all around her; her dad was a biochemistry professor, and her mom was a high school biology teacher. The influence of her parents allowed her to know from a young age that she wanted to be involved with science. She attended Cornell University to study Electrical Engineering and then transitioned to Stanford University for her master's and Ph.D. degrees.

Graduate school was one of the greatest challenges Margaret has faced. As an undergraduate, success was objectively defined by grades. In contrast, expectations in graduate school were inexplicit, with challenges such as identifying research topics, conducting experiments, and writing papers. It took time for her to learn how to frame problems and make progress on long-term projects. In graduate school, Margaret also discovered the value of having a network of female friends. At the time, women comprised less than ten percent of the engineering department. This experience encouraged the women to bond and support one another during the challenging times. Margaret commented that, "As tough as it was, I am glad I persevered because it opened up the academic career pathway that has given me so much joy."

Margaret joined the faculty at Princeton University after completing her doctoral studies and has been there ever since. During her career in academia, she has had the opportunity to teach, conduct research, and take sabbaticals across various topics. Her breadth of experiences makes her warn against stereotypes associated with science and technology. Margaret shares, "People used to think of STEM as nerdy and isolating, but I look at my life and it is richly creative and filled with so many extraordinary people to work with and become friends with too."

Iyore N. Olaye traces her interest in chemistry and engineering back to hours of her childhood spent experimenting with mixtures of household and beauty products. During this time, Iyore's mother told her stories of women and Black entrepreneurs, scientists, and intellectuals, exposing her to successful people who looked like her. Based on these experiences, it is no surprise that Iyore chose to pursue a degree in Chemical Engineering at Cornell University.

Iyore has always had an interest in digital and physical products. As a student at Cornell, Iyore participated in a fellowship for students interested in entrepreneurship, giving her the opportunity to innovate in the technology capital of the world, Silicon Valley. In the few years since her graduation, Iyore has served as the Head of Research and Development for health and beauty technology company Walker & Company Brands and is now a Product Leader at a personal transportation start-up, Bird Scooters. The fast-paced start-up environment has allowed Iyore to work on problems in areas that technology has not yet revolutionized. When asked to describe what she does, Iyore replied, "Like a conductor in an orchestra helps all the instruments blend to make beautiful music, I help teams work together to make something unique. As an engineer, I have a specialty, but I don't necessarily play all the instruments."

Iyore also has some powerful advice for younger students: "In high school, I set up rules that I now view as artificial barriers. I thought I had to go to an elite institution, graduate, and get a great job before I could focus on ideas of my own. Don't wait to innovate or explore; there is no need to. You don't want to look back and wonder what would have happened if you believed in your ambitions earlier on."

IYORE N. OLAYE

B.S. Chemical and Biomolecular Engineering, Cornell University (2016)

"Regardless of the outcome, every challenge is valuable and prepares you for your next opportunity to be victorious."

ANA PINCZUK

B.S. Mechanical Engineering, Cornell University (1984)
M.Eng. Mechanical Engineering, Cornell University (1985)
Master's in Technology Management, University of Pennsylvania (1999)
M.S. Software Management, Carnegie Mellon University (2010)

During childhood, Ana Pinczuk was accustomed to the sights and sounds of science laboratories as her parents pursued their doctoral degrees. She says, "It was never a thought, it was always math or science." What Ana knew to be an adolescent truth became a reality in adulthood. She graduated from Cornell University in Mechanical Engineering with a specific interest in robotics.

Ana went to work for AT&T Bell Laboratories, where she began as a systems engineer. Over time, she moved into various roles including running the Internet Protocol (IP) network. Since leaving AT&T, Ana has held significant management positions at Cisco Systems, Veritas Technologies, and Hewlett Packard Enterprise. She now serves as Chief Development Officer at Anaplan. Ana is passionate about bridging the gap between technology and the customers who use it. Her message: "Technology is part of every job, no matter what you do. Embed technology in everything you do."

Although she has held powerful leadership roles at many companies, Ana has faced challenges in her career. Ana left AT&T to begin her M.B.A. at Harvard Business School, but circumstances prevented her from completing her studies at Harvard. At the time, Ana thought this failure would pose an irremediable setback on her career. However, Ana quickly realized that it presented a great opportunity to try something different. "There's really nothing so bad that you can't come back from. You have to be resilient, get back up, and move forward. Be authentic and a good person. In the end, that's what really matters."

Of her time growing up in Puerto Rico, Dr. Jeannette M. Pérez-Rosselló writes, "My community of female supporters started with my grandmother, aunts, and grand-aunts." Aspiring toward a career in medicine, Jeannette left Puerto Rico to study in the College of Human Ecology at Cornell University. Despite being bilingual, Jeannette quickly discovered she could not write as well as many students and struggled to keep up with assignments. Jeannette's father also passed away during her time at Cornell, requiring her to take up a work-study job in the Admissions Office. It was through these challenges that Jeannette met many administrators and professors who served as strong mentors and encouraged her to persist through the difficulties.

Today, Jeannette is a Pediatric Radiologist at Boston Children's Hospital. Jeannette spends most of her time doing research, teaching, and speaking at conferences around the world. In medical school, Jeannette loved anatomy and discovered her strength as a visual learner, guiding her toward a specialty in radiology. Her human ecology background has led her to use science to address social issues, as Jeannette specializes in serving children who are victims of abuse. She finds the growth of children fascinating and believes that working with youth is the most rewarding career. "They're either born with [these complications], it's an accident, or it just happens. I find it much easier to work hard for that population."

Jeannette also emphasizes the importance of finding yourself a community of women, stating, "They have been especially important in giving their advice when it comes to balancing being a mother of three children and still working, teaching, and doing research."

JEANNETTE M. PÉREZ-ROSSELLÓ, M.D.

B.S. Biology and Society, Cornell University (1991)
M.D., University of Rochester School of Medicine (1995)

" When you work with sick children and see their resilience and strength, it gives you energy to work without ever worrying about the time or difficulty. "

YONN RASMUSSEN, PH.D.

B.S. Materials Science and Engineering, Cornell University (1983)
Ph.D. Materials Science and Engineering, Cornell University (1989)

Stay curious, be engaged, and pursue your dreams with confidence.

At age fifteen, Dr. Yonn Rasmussen and her family immigrated from South Korea to the United States. It was a transformative experience at an impressionable age when teenagers typically would have to cope with life adjustments that come with growing into young adulthood, even without the cultural shift. Despite the challenges she faced, Yonn focused on succeeding in school and becoming resilient, something she believes significantly helped when she encountered obstacles in future endeavors.

When Yonn was in high school, she was awarded a scholarship to participate in a Society of Women Engineers (SWE) sponsored program at the University of Maryland. As part of the program, she attended the seminar "Introduction to Careers in Engineering." She shares, "I had always excelled in math and science, but through this program, I learned about each type of engineering field and became very interested in majoring in engineering in college." She visited Cornell University as a prospective student, quickly fell in love with the school, and was soon a part of Cornell's SWE section.

Yonn began her engineering career as a technical specialist and project manager with Xerox. Over time she has gained experience spanning research, technology development, product design, and manufacturing. Her vast range of knowledge launched her into a Vice President position within Xerox. With Yonn's leadership, scientists and engineers at Xerox integrate technology with product development to increase efficiency as well as bring value to society. Yonn shares, "I like to see the science in the laboratory being developed into new technology and eventually becoming products in the marketplace, touching people's lives in a positive and productive way."

Danielle Regis grew up in a household that embraced engineering and math. Her parents taught her that no matter how challenging a subject appeared, it was conquerable. Equipped with this mindset, Danielle thrived when faced with challenges as a child. She liked to take things apart, understand how they worked, and put them back together. When she discovered there was a whole career path centered around solving problems, she was eager to become an engineer.

During her first year at Cornell University, while handing in her calculus homework, Danielle asked Electrical and Computer Engineering (ECE) professor Bruce Land to borrow his stapler. Through this simple interaction and the conversation that ensued, she learned about the ECE major and was soon convinced it was for her. ECE gave her the tools to explore technology, flexibility in her career, and more opportunities than she knew existed. While the promises of what ECE had in store were exciting, the reality of the major proved to be challenging beyond her imagination. Not only was the material complex, but she also had a tough time adjusting to being the only Black woman in the major. She ultimately had to develop a great amount of inner strength and confidence to acknowledge that there was no shame to admitting that she could not make it through the major alone. She found the greatest fulfillment and success when she learned to lean on others for help and provide the same support to others. The journey was long and hard, but she would never change it because it helped her develop into the engineer and empathetic leader she is today. Sophomore year, Danielle landed a summer internship with the Federal Government and has continued to do mission-critical work ever since.

In her free time, Danielle gives back by leading coding classes and other STEM education programs for underrepresented demographics with a company called STEMBoard. In the classroom, she leverages every intersection of her identity to ensure that her students develop an unflappable sense of belonging in STEM fields.

DANIELLE REGIS

B.S. Electrical and Computer Engineering, Cornell University (2015)
M.Eng. Electrical and Computer Engineering, Cornell University (2016)

"A career in STEM gives you the ability to have an impact on the world in ways that are unparalleled."

HILARY LASHLEY RENISON

B.S. Mechanical and Aerospace Engineering, Cornell University (2005)
M.S. Mechanical Engineering, Cornell University (2007)
M.B.A., Cornell University (2009)

" On my twelfth birthday, I had my first flight lesson. It was the most amazing experience, and, just like that, I was sold on the power of technology. "

Growing up, Hilary Lashley Renison had a fascination with airplanes and aspirations of becoming a commercial airline pilot. Hilary was part of a special high school program in Farmingdale, New York, where she attended traditional classes in the morning and spent the afternoons taking flight lessons. As the only female in the program, Hilary says, "I found myself often being very isolated, so I dug deeper into my studies." Hilary graduated high school at age sixteen and entered Cornell University's Mechanical and Aerospace Engineering program.

Hilary broadened her passion for technologies that change the world while at Cornell. After graduating with her third degree from Cornell University in 2009, she travelled to India to join a start-up company working to create solar-powered point-of-use products for rural areas. When asked about her biggest takeaway from this experience, Hilary said, "Being outside of my comfort zone, I learned a ton about myself and how important it is to leverage customers as partners in your product development journey." Today, Hilary is a Senior Business Development Manager at General Electric's Research Center, supporting the commercialization of cutting-edge technologies in aviation, energy, and healthcare.

In addition to her role at General Electric, Hilary founded Tinker & Fiddle, an organization that provides children, particularly from underrepresented backgrounds, with access to science and technology education. Hilary wants to play a part in increasing the diversity of the technical workforce. She writes, "We all have blind spots, and if we keep the technical conversations monochromatic, we are not going to get solutions that meet the needs of everyone."

From the moment Sonya Sephaban saw the first man step onto the moon in 1969, she was determined to become an astronaut. After college, Sonya started her career at NASA, where she repeatedly applied to become an astronaut, making it further in the process with each application. Although she was not selected as an astronaut candidate, she remained motivated and began an extensive career in the aerospace industry.

In 2009, Sonya made the transition from Northrop Grumman in Los Angeles, California to General Dynamics in Detroit, Michigan. Sonya's job was to accelerate the development of rough-terrain military vehicles, an area vastly different from her past work in space technology. It was in this role that Sonya noticed the severe dearth of women in technical positions. Sonya recalls having to look five levels down in the organization to find another woman or individual from a diverse background. When Sonya retired from General Dynamics, she decided to commit her time to building inclusive workplace cultures. As co-founder and Chief Executive Officer of the software company, OurOffice, Inc., she has helped to develop the first technology platform and turnkey solution for building inclusive workplace cultures.

Despite her passion for promoting diversity and inclusion, Sonya has encountered her fair share of doubters. When asked how she approaches these difficult conversations, Sonya remarked, "Diversity and inclusion is about allowance. More than tolerance, allowance is truly being okay with everyone's opinions and perspectives, including people who are against diversity and inclusion. You have to have compassion, understanding, and allowance for people that doubt you."

SONYA SEPAHBAN

B.S. Chemical Engineering, Cornell University (1982)
M.S. Chemical Engineering, Rice University (1985)
M.B.A., University of Houston (1989)

66 If anything, it's an advantage to be a woman. 99

JACLYN A. SPEAR

B.S. Electrical Engineering, Cornell University (1975)
M.B.A., University of Pittsburgh (1985)

An engineering degree opens the doors to just about anything you want to do with your life.

Jaclyn A. Spear grew up in a family of Cornell University engineers, so it was no surprise that she followed in both of her parents' footsteps, studying Electrical Engineering at Cornell University. At that time, there were only fifty female students enrolled in the College of Engineering and no female faculty. Despite some personal academic challenges she faced and the dearth of women, Jaclyn was instrumental in chartering the university's Society of Women Engineers (SWE) section. Jaclyn recognizes the opportunities that having an engineering degree can offer to women and believes SWE offers women a supportive community and leadership opportunities.

Jaclyn's involvement with SWE continued to grow after college. While working in various field service and project management roles in the nuclear power industry, Jaclyn served as the National SWE President from 1994-95. Jaclyn later took a year-long leave of absence for a position through the Institute of Electrical and Electronics Engineers Government Fellows Program as a congressional staffer with the House Foreign Relations Committee. In this position, she learned about how the issues she was working on from an engineering standpoint were being considered from a legislative perspective.

Throughout her forty-two-year career, Jaclyn has sustained an excitement to learn new things, meet new people, and share new ideas. When asked for wisdom based on her long career in engineering, Jaclyn offered, "Be a jack-of-all trades and a generalist! If they're looking for volunteers to go do something, volunteer! It may be a career changer, and you may not realize that until you try new things."

Elissa Sterry embraces variety and diversity in both her professional and personal life and has always strived to live her life to the fullest. After graduating from the Operations Research program at Cornell University, Elissa accepted a job with ExxonMobil. In 2006, Elissa became the first female Vice President of ExxonMobil Chemical Company, a position she would hold for eleven years before retiring in 2017.

Throughout her career, Elissa worked to create a positive and encouraging atmosphere in which employees from all backgrounds could flourish. When Elissa started at ExxonMobil, there was no community of women, but she was accepted as "one of the boys." Today, ExxonMobil is enormously diverse, including a large community of women. Elissa was proud to see this culture evolve and personally found it very fulfilling to give people who were previously overlooked, or who didn't conform to a particular style, a chance to grow within the company. Elissa, like many others, has struggled to be accepted for what she can contribute but advises that having "courage of conviction" is key.

Elissa remains busy in retirement and continues to build upon the hobbies she began to explore while at Exxon. Elissa has always emphasized the importance of pursuing interests outside of the technical world. Today, you can find Elissa on the ballroom dance floor or in the wine tasting room as she practices her certified sommelier skills. Elissa continues to serve her communities through Battlefield Leadership, a consulting group that uses historical battles to teach modern leadership skills, and through her position on the Cornell Engineering College Council.

ELISSA STERRY

B.S. Operations Research and Information Engineering, Cornell University (1979)
M.Eng. Operations Research and Information Engineering, Cornell University (1980)

66 Never be afraid to ask. The simple act of asking people their thoughts can open a door and create the opportunity for an eye-opening conversation and relationship. 99

JILL CORNELL TARTER, PH.D.

B.S. Engineering Physics, Cornell University (1966)
M.A. Astronomy, University of California, Berkeley (1971)
Ph.D. Astronomy, University of California, Berkeley (1975)

When Dr. Jill Cornell Tarter was eight years old, she declared she would be an engineer. However, when Jill completed her engineering degree at Cornell University, she realized that although she received an invaluable education in problem solving, engineering was not her calling.

Jill's journey at Cornell in the 1960s was strikingly different from that of today's engineering students. Women were confined to their dormitories from ten in the evening to six in the morning and were required to wear skirts whenever making the trek from their dormitories to campus. Jill faced an extreme culture of prejudice against women; she was only allowed to be an 'honorary' member of Tau Beta Pi, the engineering honor society, and was asked not to attend a nuclear physics lecture the day the professor discussed how radiation causes sterility. Women were excluded from teamwork, leaving Jill to tackle her homework independently, yet she persevered and soon found her niche. Jill advises, "Find something that you can do better than anyone else, then use this skill to solve all sorts of problems you find interesting, even if nobody has thought to do that before."

In her last semester at Cornell, Jill discovered a newfound interest in astronomy after enrolling in a star formation course. Inspiration from this class led her to study astronomy in graduate school and later co-found the Search for Extraterrestrial Intelligence (SETI) Institute, where she now serves as Chair Emeritus for SETI Research. Jill's profession allows her to explore profound questions surrounding the origin of life and the evolution of intelligence. "For me personally, detection of an extraterrestrial technological civilization would mean that we Earthlings can have a long future."

Carole Rapp Thompson has always loved numbers. As a student at Cornell University, she ranked statistics among her favorite coursework. Carole remarks, "At that time, women were considered inferior in math. In the 1950s, the government was virtually the only source of 'equal pay for equal work' for women." With these challenges, Carole pursued a career in government, after passing the Federal Service Entrance Examination.

After graduation, Carole joined the Bureau of Labor Statistics in the U.S. Department of Labor. While working on the Bureau's Occupational Outlook Handbook, a publication aimed at funneling high school students into areas of economic growth, she learned about the "brand new" field of computer programming. Recognizing the potential in this field, Carole challenged herself and became the second computer programmer in the Bureau of Labor Statistics. Later, she worked as both a systems and management analyst at the U.S. Agency for International Development and the administrative office of the Peace Corps.

In 1965, Carole pursued a role at the United Nations (U.N.), working as a programmer and data analyst in the Statistical Office. Carole remembers that her new colleagues were surprised by the extent of her experience and resented the grade level at which she entered. At that time "almost no one, let alone a woman, had seven years of programming experience." She transferred to the Department of Administration and Management and was eventually promoted to Director of the Electronic Services Division. Here, her work included overseeing the establishment and operation of a global telecommunications network, as well as responsibility for office automation and mainframe computer activities at the U.N. headquarters and at the major regional offices. By her retirement in 1995, Carole had risen in the ranks at the U.N. and witnessed the transformation and adoption of technology over the course of her career.

CAROLE RAPP THOMPSON

B.S. Industrial and Labor Relations, Cornell University (1956)

> In the course of my career, especially in the early years, I was usually the only woman in the room. This experience led me to mentor the younger women who worked with and under me.

PORTIA YARBOROUGH, PH.D.

B.S. Chemistry, Wake Forest University (1993)
M.S. Polymer Chemistry, Cornell University (1996)
Ph.D. Polymer Chemistry, Cornell University (1998)

"My curiosity for science was sparked, and, ever since that [high school chemistry] class, I have had an insatiable drive to learn more about the world around me."

Dr. Portia Yarborough has worked to advance the science and application of high-performance engineered polymers to create essential innovations for leading industries. This love for chemistry and materials was sparked by one of her high school teachers, Mr. Knox, who introduced her to the world of electrons and orbital fields. Although Portia entered the workforce with significant technical achievements, she quickly recognized that success is more about how you respond to the changes around you. Having a mindset to always see the opportunity in challenges, she uses this perspective in cultivating global teams to advance science across all sectors and applications. Portia shares, "Emotional intelligence, how you interact with others, and building lasting networks have been key factors for success in my career at DuPont."

Portia also notes the importance of female role models who were instrumental in her professional growth and development. Whether that was mentors who guided Portia through her time at Cornell University or the female leaders at work who shared their own lessons with younger employees, Portia found these relationships invaluable and, as a result, nurtured lifelong relationships. "Building a network of trusted advisors was useful for navigating the playing field, giving me courage to step into new experiences and, ultimately, enabling my growth into an effective leader."

When Portia was asked who inspired her, she said, "I am inspired by the passion and energy of the younger generation who are using their voice to raise awareness of sustainability. Collectively, we can make a positive impact on the world through science."

MEET THE AUTHORS

MADELINE DUBELIER
B.S. Mechanical Engineering, Cornell University (2020)
Cornell SWE Co-President FY20

CATHERINE GURECKY
B.S. Chemical Engineering, Cornell University (2020)
M.Eng. Chemical Engineering, Cornell University (2020)
Cornell SWE Co-President FY20

ABIGAIL MACALUSO
B.S. Operations Research & Information Engineering,
Cornell University (2020)
Cornell SWE Member

The Cornell University section of the Society of Women Engineers (SWE) was chartered on November 9, 1972. The award-winning Cornell SWE section promotes women in engineering by advocating the importance of diversity in technical fields and by uniting resources to encourage academic, professional, and personal excellence. For many years, outreach in the local and national communities has been a cornerstone of Cornell SWE's mission, reaching hundreds of elementary, middle, and high school students each year.

All net proceeds from this publication will support Cornell SWE outreach initiatives aimed at inspiring the next generation of scientists and engineers.

PORTRAITS BY

DAVID ROSS JANSEN

B.A. Performing and Media Arts – Film Concentration,
Cornell University (2022)

CPSIA information can be obtained
at www.ICGtesting.com
Printed in the USA
BVHW021719050820
585564BV00002B/9